HOW LONG, GREAT PUMPKIN, HOW LONG?

Peanuts Parade Paperbacks

HOW LONG, GREAT PUMPKIN, HOW LONG?

Cartoons from *You're the Guest of Honor, Charlie Brown* and *Win a Few, Lose a Few, Charlie Brown*

by Charles M. Schulz

Holt, Rinehart and Winston / New York

Published simultaneously in Canada by Holt, Rinehart
and Winston of Canada, Limited.

First published in this form in 1977.

Library of Congress Catalog Card Number: 76-43502

ISBN: 0-03-020661-8

Printed in the United States of America

10 9 8 7 6 5 4 3 2 1

The Bunnies - A Tale of Mirth and Woe.

"Ha Ha Ha," laughed the bunnies.

"Ha Ha Ha Ha Ha Ha Ha Ha Ha Ha Ha Ha"

SO MUCH FOR THE MIRTH!

SLEEPING AGAIN

I DON'T SEE WHY YOU NEED SO MUCH REST

I NEED PLENTY OF REST IN CASE TOMORROW IS A GREAT DAY..

IT PROBABLY WON'T BE, BUT IF IT IS, I'LL BE READY!

WOODSTOCK IS REALLY INTO HOPSCOTCH

CLICK! PLUNK!

HEE HEE HEE HEE HEE

STUPID BIRD!

WHAT'S SO GREAT ABOUT WINNING THIRTY GAMES OF EIGHT-BALL IN A ROW?

HEE HEE HEE HEE

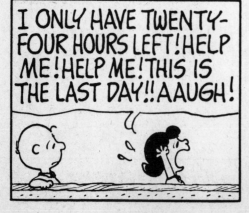

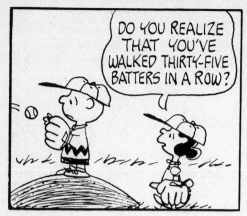

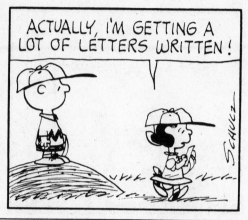

Dear Contributor,
We regret to inform you that your manuscript does not suit our present needs. The Editors

STOMP! STOMP! STOMP! STOMP!

WHAM!

P.S. Don't take it out on your mailbox.

I FIND IT DIFFICULT TO BELIEVE THAT GOD REALLY CARES WHO WINS A GOLF TOURNAMENT!

MY DAD IS PLAYING IN A CANCER FUND GOLF TOURNAMENT TOMORROW...

MY MOM IS PLAYING IN A TENNIS TOURNAMENT NEXT WEEK FOR THE KIDNEY FOUNDATION...

WE SHOULD HOLD A BENEFIT BASEBALL TOURNAMENT

THAT'S A GREAT IDEA!

I CAN SEE IT NOW... "CHARLIE BROWN'S FLU TOURNAMENT!"

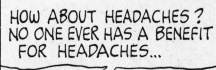

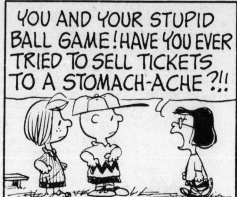

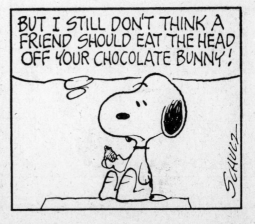

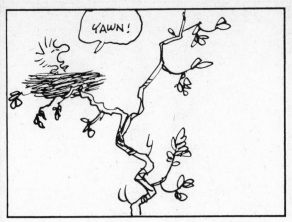

"Hi, pretty girl," he said.

"I love you," she said, and together they laughed. Then one day she said, "I hate you," and they cried. But not together.

"What happened to the love that we said would never die?" she asked. "It died," he said.

The first time he saw her she was playing tennis. The last time he saw her she was playing tennis.

"Ours was a Love set," he said, "but we double-faulted." "You always talked a better game than you played," she said.

THAT'S VERY GOOD...NOW ALL YOU NEED IS A TITLE...

A Love Story
by Erich Beagle

Dear Contributor,
We are returning your stupid story.

You are a terrible writer. Why do you bother us? We wouldn't buy one of your stories if you paid us.

Leave us alone. Drop dead. Get lost.

PROBABLY A FORM REJECTION SLIP...

flitter
flitter
flutter
flitter

flitter
flitter
SPUT
SPUT
flutter
flutter
SPUT
SPUT
SPUT

BOING!!

EJECTED JUST IN TIME!

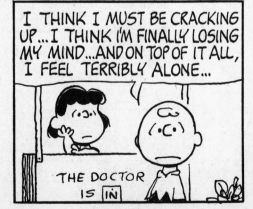

PSYCHIATRIC HELP 5¢

YESTERDAY MORNING I WOKE UP VERY EARLY...I JUST COULDN'T SLEEP...

THE DOCTOR IS IN

MY BEDROOM FACES EAST, AND SO I COULD SEE THE SUN COMING UP...ONLY, IT WASN'T THE SUN... IT WAS A HUGE **BASEBALL**!

I THINK I MUST BE CRACKING UP...I THINK I'M FINALLY LOSING MY MIND...AND ON TOP OF IT ALL, I FEEL TERRIBLY ALONE...

THE DOCTOR IS IN

OKAY, NOW TELL ME MORE ABOUT THIS HUGE BASEBALL..

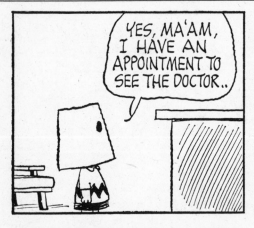

WHAT ARE YOU PACKING FOR, BIG BROTHER?

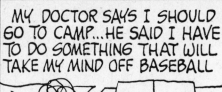

MY DOCTOR SAYS I SHOULD GO TO CAMP...HE SAID I HAVE TO DO SOMETHING THAT WILL TAKE MY MIND OFF BASEBALL

I'VE SEEN YOU PLAY.. I NEVER THOUGHT YOU HAD YOUR MIND ON IT!

THANKS A LOT... I'LL SEE YOU IN TWO WEEKS...

YOU'RE GOING TO BE A BIG HIT AT CAMP CARRYING YOUR HEAD IN A SACK!!

SCHULZ

SO HERE I AM ON A BUS GOING TO CAMP...

FOR SOMEONE WHO HATES GOING TO CAMP, I SURE SPEND A LOT OF TIME THERE...MAYBE I WENT TO THE WRONG DOCTOR...

EVERY SUMMER HE DRAGS HIS FAMILY OFF ON A FIVE-WEEK CAMPING TRIP...HIS SOLUTION FOR EVERYTHING IS "GO TO CAMP!"

I KNOW WHAT'LL HAPPEN TO ME.. JUST WHEN I GET OLD ENOUGH WHERE I WON'T HAVE TO GO ANY MORE, I'LL GET DRAFTED INTO THE INFANTRY!

SCHULZ

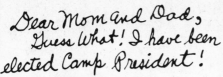

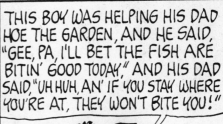

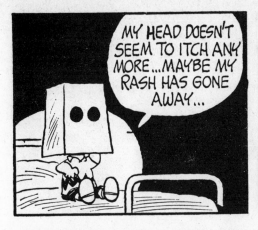

MY HEAD DOESN'T SEEM TO ITCH ANY MORE...MAYBE MY RASH HAS GONE AWAY...

IF IT HAS, I COULD TAKE THIS STUPID GROCERY SACK OFF MY HEAD...OF COURSE, THEN I PROBABLY WOULDN'T BE CAMP PRESIDENT ANY MORE, EITHER...

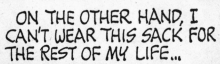

ON THE OTHER HAND, I CAN'T WEAR THIS SACK FOR THE REST OF MY LIFE...

IF I EVER WENT TO A GROCERY STORE, AND THE CLERK YELLED, "CARRY OUT!" I'D END UP IN THE BACK OF SOME STATION WAGON!

PSST, MR. SACK... WHAT ARE YOU DOING UP SO EARLY?

I'M GOING OUT TO WATCH THE SUN RISE...IF IT'S THE SUN, I'LL KNOW I'M CURED...IF IT'S A BASEBALL, I'M STILL IN TROUBLE..

?? HE DIDN'T HAVE A SACK OVER HIS HEAD ??!??

HE IS OUR CAMP PRESIDENT ?!?

ANOTHER GAME TODAY...IF WE WIN, WE'LL ONLY BE TEN GAMES OUT OF SEVENTH PLACE...

WHY DO YOU ALWAYS PUT YOUR LEFT SHOE ON FIRST, BIG BROTHER?

WELL, ACTUALLY, I DON'T...I ONLY PUT IT ON FIRST ON DAYS WHEN WE HAVE A BASEBALL GAME...

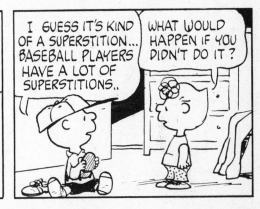

I GUESS IT'S KIND OF A SUPERSTITION... BASEBALL PLAYERS HAVE A LOT OF SUPERSTITIONS..

WHAT WOULD HAPPEN IF YOU DIDN'T DO IT?

WELL, WE'D PROBABLY LOSE THE GAME

HAVE YOU EVER WON?

WHERE'S OUR PITCHER?

I DON'T KNOW...I HAVEN'T SEEN HIM..

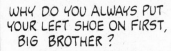

!?

I DON'T UNDERSTAND...THE GAME IS READY TO START, AND YOU'RE STILL SITTING HERE IN YOUR BEDROOM WITHOUT YOUR SHOES ON!

I'VE NEVER SEEN IT TO FAIL!

FIND A GOOD SPOT, AND EVERYONE ELSE MOVES IN!

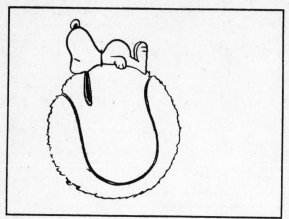

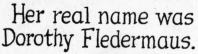
I CAN'T SLEEP LIKE THAT...

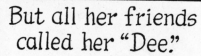
ALL THE BLOOD RUSHES TO MY NOSE!

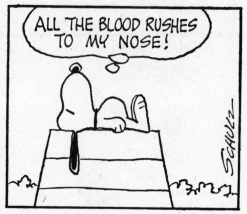

Her real name was Dorothy Fledermaus.

But all her friends called her "Dee."

Thus, she was frequently referred to as "Dee Fledermaus."

UH UH!

THAT JUST DOESN'T WORK..

I HAVE TO SLEEP IN THE SAME DIRECTION THAT THE WORLD TURNS

I HATE SLEEPING IN WOODSTOCK'S GUEST ROOM!

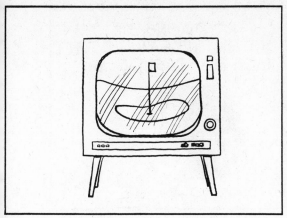

ALL RIGHT, GOLF FANS, THIS IS IT...THE OLD PRO HAS TO MAKE THIS ONE...

HE'S DOWN TO THE LAST PUTT, AND HE CAN'T PLAY IT SAFE...HE HAS TO GO FOR IT...

THERE'S NO TOMORROW!

THERE'S NO TOMORROW?!

THERE'S NO TOMORROW!!

THEY JUST ANNOUNCED ON TV THAT THERE'S **NO** TOMORROW!!!

THERE'S NO TOMORROW!! THEY JUST ANNOUNCED IT ON TV!

PANIC! PANIC! RUN! HIDE! FLEE! RUN FOR THE HILLS! FLEE TO THE VALLEYS! RUN TO THE ROOF TOPS!

SOMEHOW I NEVER THOUGHT IT WOULD END THIS WAY!

I THOUGHT ELIJAH WAS TO COME FIRST...

Though her husband often went on business trips, she hated to be left alone.

"I've solved our problem," he said. "I've bought you a St. Bernard. It's name is Great Reluctance."

"Now, when I go away, you shall know that I am leaving you with Great Reluctance!"

She hit him with a waffle iron.

OVERHEAD SMASH!

YES, SIR

IF YOU'RE NOT FEELING WELL, THE VET SAID I SHOULD TAKE YOUR TEMPERATURE, AND THEN CALL HIM BACK...

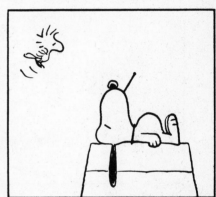

THAT'S FUNNY... ACCORDING TO THIS, YOUR TEMPERATURE IS ONLY FORTY-TWO...

I DON'T UNDERSTAND

SOMEBODY MUST HAVE HAD COLD FEET!

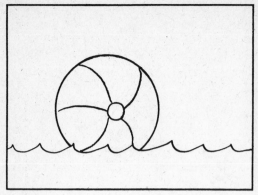

BABE RUTH HIT SEVEN HUNDRED AND FOURTEEN HOME RUNS...

THAT HAS TO BE ONE OF THE MOST FANTASTIC RECORDS IN THE HISTORY OF SPORTS...

BUT SNOOPY HAS HIT SEVEN HUNDRED AND THIRTEEN HOME RUNS! HE ONLY NEEDS ONE MORE TO TIE THE RECORD...

JUST A LITTLE OL' COUNTRY BOY DOIN' HIS JOB!

STRIKE THREE!

IF YOU'RE GOING TO BREAK BABE RUTH'S HOME-RUN RECORD, YOU'RE GOING TO HAVE TO DO BETTER THAN THAT...

AS YOU SEEM TO KNOW...

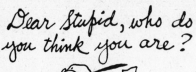

Dear Stupid, who do you think you are?

If you break the Babe's home run record, we'll break you! We'll run you out of the country! We hate your kind!

IS YOUR HATE MAIL CAUSING YOU TO LOSE ANY SLEEP?

ONLY WHEN IT FALLS ON ME

THIS IS OUR LAST GAME OF THE SEASON, SNOOPY...

IF YOU DON'T HIT A HOME RUN TODAY AND TIE BABE RUTH'S RECORD, HANK AARON WILL BEAT YOU TO IT!

TOUGH LUCK, HANK... I'M GOING TO HIT THE FIRST PITCH OVER THE FENCE...

WELL, MAYBE THE SECOND PITCH...

STRIKE THREE!

DON'T WORRY, SNOOPY, YOU'LL GET TO BAT AT LEAST TWO MORE TIMES...

BY THE WAY, TEETH MARKS ARE NOT GOOD FOR YOUR BAT...

ALL RIGHT, SNOOPY, IT'S THE NINTH INNING...

THIS WILL BE YOUR LAST TIME AT BAT THIS SEASON...IF YOU'RE GOING TO TIE BABE RUTH'S HOME-RUN RECORD, YOU'VE GOT TO DO IT NOW!

CHARLIE BROWN'S ON SECOND... A HOME RUN WILL TIE THE RECORD AND WIN THE GAME! IT'S HERO TIME, SNOOPY!!

I JUST WANT TO BE A CREDIT TO MY BREED!

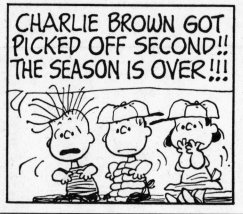

I'M SORRY, SNOOPY...I KNOW I SPOILED YOUR CHANCE TO TIE BABE RUTH'S RECORD...

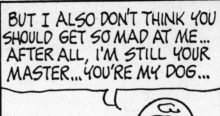

BUT I ALSO DON'T THINK YOU SHOULD GET SO MAD AT ME... AFTER ALL, I'M STILL YOUR MASTER...YOU'RE MY DOG...

JUST REMEMBER, ONE LITTLE PHONE CALL AND I COULD HAVE YOU SENT RIGHT BACK WHERE YOU CAME FROM!

Z

Z

POOF!

Z Z

Their Love Was Not in the Cards

"You've always ignored me," she said. "And now you say you want to marry me."

"Every night you play cards."

"I'm really afraid," she said, "that you love cards more than you love me."

"If you could say something nice to me just once, perhaps I'd marry you."

" ◇ ♣ ♡ ♠ "

"You blew it!" she said, and walked out of his life forever.

Gentlemen, I have just completed my new novel.

It is so good, I am not even going to send it to you.

Why don't you just come and get it?

Gentlemen,

Yesterday, I waited all day for you to come and get my novel and to publish it and make me rich and famous.

You did not show up.

Were you not feeling well?

Gentlemen,

Well, another day has gone by and you still haven't come to pick up my novel for publication.

Just for that, I am going to offer it to another publisher.

Nyahh! Nyahh! Nyahh!

RATS!

IT'S HOPELESS!

IF I'M GOING TO WORK AT NIGHT, I'M GOING TO HAVE TO HAVE AN INDOOR STUDIO...

YOU CAN'T WRITE BY FIREFLY!!

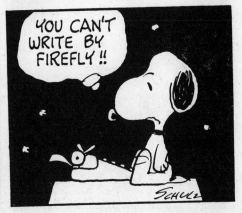

Theme: Our School

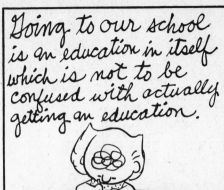

Going to our school is an education in itself which is not to be confused with actually getting an education.

I DON'T NEED THAT KIND OF TROUBLE!

MISS OTHMAR...

IF I WERE TO BRING A TV DINNER TO SCHOOL TOMORROW, WOULD I BE ALLOWED TO USE ONE OF THE OVENS IN THE CAFETERIA TO HEAT IT UP?

I SEE

HAVE YOU EVER NOTICED HOW A CERTAIN KIND OF QUESTION TENDS TO UPSET HER?

BLEAH!

SOMEBODY'S ALWAYS STIRRING UP THE ENEMY!

His wife had always hated his work.

"You'll never make any money growing toadstools," she complained.

"On the contrary," he declared. "My toadstool business is mushrooming!"

She creamed him with the electric toaster.

"Do you love me?" she asked.
"Of course," he said.

"Do you really love me?" she asked.
"Of course," he said.

"Do you really really love me?" she asked.
"No," he said.

"Do you love me?" she asked.
"Of course," he said.
So she asked no more.

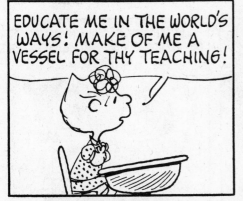

GOOD MORNING, MISS... I'M SELLING A NEW ITEM FOR KITTENS, AND I..

FOR WHAT?

FOR KITTENS...THIS IS A NEW TOY I HAVE DEVELOPED...A KITTEN CAN ENTERTAIN HIMSELF FOR HOURS WITH THIS TOY...

THE TOY IS SIMPLICITY ITSELF... I HAVE TAKEN SEVERAL PIECES OF SCRAP PAPER AND I HAVE CRUMPLED THEM UP...

A KITTEN WILL PLAY FOR HOURS WITH A PIECE OF CRUMPLED PAPER! HE'LL BAT IT, AND HE'LL JUMP AT IT...

AND IF YOU HANG IT FROM A STRING, HE'LL HIT IT AND BOX WITH IT AND EVERYTHING!

IT'S REALLY FUN TO WATCH A KITTEN BOUNCE AROUND...

WOULD YOU LIKE TO BUY ONE? THEY'RE ONLY FIVE CENTS APIECE..

WHY SHOULD I BUY ONE? WHY CAN'T I JUST CRUMPLE A PIECE OF PAPER MYSELF?

ALL ALONG I'VE BEEN AFRAID THERE WAS SOMETHING WRONG WITH THIS IDEA...

I DON'T KNOW WHAT'S WRONG WITH MY PASS RECEIVER...HE KEEPS COMPLAINING ABOUT HEADACHES...

GOOD MORNING, CHUCK...BOY, WAS THAT EVER A LONG NIGHT!

WHAT I NEED IS A ROUSING BREAKFAST...

HOW ABOUT A STACK OF HOT CAKES WITH TWO FRIED EGGS, SOME SAUSAGE, ORANGE JUICE AND A SLICE OF MELON?

WHICH KIND OF COLD CEREAL WOULD YOU LIKE?

YES, MA'AM...I'D LIKE TO TRANSFER TEMPORARILY TO YOUR SCHOOL..

MY DAD IS OUT OF TOWN, YOU SEE, AND I'M STAYING IN CHUCK'S GUEST COTTAGE SO I'LL BE GOING TO THIS SCHOOL FOR AWHILE IF YOU'LL HAVE ME...OKAY?

I'M NO GREAT SCHOLAR, YOU UNDERSTAND, BUT I'M ALWAYS IN THERE TRYING...

IF IT'S "TRUE OR FALSE" OR "MULTIPLE CHOICE," I'LL BE IN THERE WITH THE BEST OF 'EM!

"Our love will last forever," he said.

"Oh, yes, yes, yes!" she cried.

"Forever being a relative term, however," he said.

She hit him with a ski pole.

YOU CAN'T SLEEP ON A COLD NOSE!

The last car drove away. It began to rain.

And so our hero's life ended as it had begun... a disaster.

"I never got any breaks," he had always complained.

He had wanted to be rich. He died poor. He wanted friends. He died friendless.

He wanted to be loved. He died unloved. He wanted laughter. He found only tears.

He wanted applause. He received boos. He wanted fame. He found only obscurity. He wanted answers. He found only questions.

I'M HAVING A HARD TIME ENDING THIS..

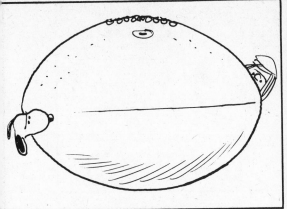

THIS IS WHAT HAPPENS ON HALLOWEEN NIGHT, MARCIE...

THE GREAT PUMPKIN RISES OUT OF THE PUMPKIN PATCH, AND FLIES THROUGH THE AIR AND BRINGS TOYS TO ALL THE CHILDREN IN THE WORLD!

I'VE HEARD ABOUT YOU

SIR, DO YOU BELIEVE IN THE GREAT PUMPKIN?

THE GREAT WHAT?

LINUS SAYS THERE'S A GREAT PUMPKIN WHO BRINGS US TOYS ON HALLOWEEN NIGHT

THE WORLD IS FILLED WITH WEIRD PEOPLE, MARCIE...

I'M FINDING THAT OUT, SIR!

BONK!

WOODSTOCK MAKES A LOUSY FALCON!

Z

AHEM!

THIS IS A TERRIBLE PROGRAM... WE SHOULD SWITCH CHANNELS

CLICK!

THAT WAS PRETTY GOOD CONSIDERING HE NEVER EVEN WOKE UP!

This is my report on rain. Rain is water which does not come out of faucets.

If it were not for rain, we would not get wet walking to school and get a sore throat and stay home which is not a bad idea.

Rain was the inspiration for that immortal poem, "Rain, rain, go away. Come again some other day."

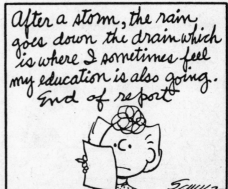
After a storm, the rain goes down the drain which is where I sometimes feel my education is also going. End of report

She wanted to live in Canada.

He wanted to live in Mexico. Thus, they parted.

Years later, when asked the reason, she replied simply,

"I just didn't like his latitude!"

IT'S ALWAYS THE SAME...

HELLO AND GOODBY!

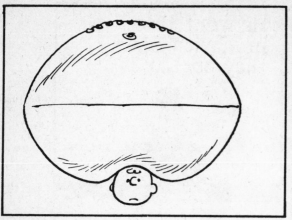

THINGS LIKE THAT COULD RUIN SPECTATOR SPORTS...

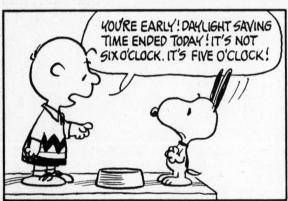

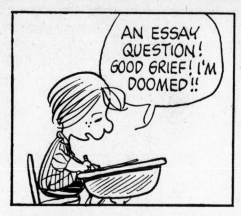

DO YOU THINK THAT LIFE HAS ITS PEAKS AND VALLEYS?

YES, I'M SURE THAT IT HAS

THEN, THAT MEANS THAT THERE MUST BE ONE DAY ABOVE ALL OTHERS IN EACH LIFE THAT IS THE HAPPIEST, RIGHT?

YES, I GUESS THAT'S PROBABLY TRUE...

WHAT IF YOU'VE ALREADY HAD IT?

Book One
Part I
Chapter One
Page 1.

WHAT A GREAT START!

HERE'S THE TEAM DOCTOR TROTTING OUT ONTO THE FIELD TO AID A DISTRESSED PLAYER...

HMM...

OBVIOUSLY A SIMPLE CASE OF HYPONATREMIA

ALL HE NEEDS IS A LITTLE WATER AND A LITTLE SALT...

 They had named their Great Dane "Good Authority."

 One day, she asked her husband if he had seen her new belt.

 "Belt?" he said. "Oh, I'm sorry. I thought it was a dog collar. I have it on Good Authority."

 Shortly thereafter, their marriage began to go downhill.

 I THINK YOUR STORIES ARE STUPID!

 IF THEY'RE EVER PRINTED IN A BOOK, I REFUSE TO WASTE MY MONEY ON IT...

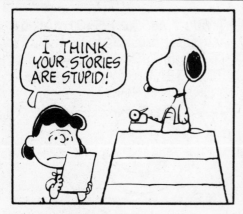 HOWEVER, IF YOU GET SOME FREE AUTHOR'S COPIES, I'LL BE GLAD TO TAKE ONE!

 BONK!

IF HE TRIES TO INSTALL A CABLE CAR AND A SUMMIT RESTAURANT, I'M LEAVING!

HERE WE ARE SKATING OUT ONTO WOODSTOCK'S HOME ICE FOR THE BIG HOCKEY GAME...

AND HERE COME THE OFFICIALS...

THE REFEREE

THE LINESMEN

THE GOAL JUDGES AND THE PENALTY TIMEKEEPER

THE OFFICIAL SCORER AND THE GAME TIMEKEEPER!

WHICH BRINGS UP A SLIGHT PROBLEM...

WHERE DO WE PUT THE ORGAN FOR THE NATIONAL ANTHEM?

SCHULZ

Winter had come again all too soon, and it was time for Joe Jacket to bring in his polar cows.

As he rode out from the barn, the first flakes of snow began to fall.

He looked up at the slate-gray sky and shivered.

The blizzard started quickly. A howling wind pounded the snow across the bleak prairie.

Joe Jacket hunched forward in the saddle, and urged his mount forward through the flying snow and screaming wind.

TELL MY PUBLISHERS NOT TO EXPECT A MANUSCRIPT UNTIL SPRING!

ALL RIGHT! CUT IT OUT!!

YOU CAN STOP DOING THAT ANY TIME!

I SAID CUT IT OUT!!

I KNOW WHAT YOU'RE UP TO!

SHE WANTS TO BE THE TALLEST ONE IN OUR FAMILY...

EVERY TIME SHE WALKS BY, SHE PUSHES DOWN ON MY HEAD TO KEEP ME FROM GROWING!

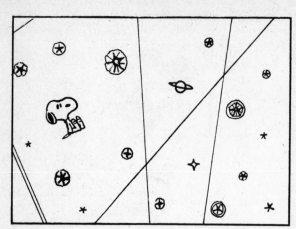

I'M READY!

SO IT'S "SHOW AND TELL" TIME AGAIN, IS IT? WELL, DO I EVER HAVE A SURPRISE FOR YOU TODAY!

I HAVE A LITTLE FILM TO SHOW YOU THAT'S GONNA KNOCK YOUR EYES OUT!

NO, MA'AM... THAT'S ONLY AN EXPRESSION..

ALL RIGHT, IF I CAN HAVE A COUPLE OF YOU STRONG TYPES LIFT THIS PROJECTOR INTO PLACE, WE CAN GET THIS SHOW ON THE ROAD!

NO, LET'S PUT IT ON THAT TABLE BACK THERE... HOW ABOUT YOU FOUR WEIRDOS MOVING THAT TABLE?

AND I'LL NEED A COUPLE MORE TO PUT THIS SCREEN UP... LET'S GO!! ON THE DOUBLE, THERE!

STRETCH THAT CORD ACROSS THE BACK, AND PLUG IT INTO THAT SOCKET IN THE CORNER...

OKAY, SOMEONE RUN DOWN TO THE CUSTODIAN THEN, AND GET AN EXTENSION! YOU THERE, GET GOING!!

NOW, WHAT ABOUT THOSE WINDOW SHADES? LET'S HAVE ALL OF YOU WHO SIT ALONG THE SIDE THERE PULL DOWN THOSE STUPID SHADES..

AND I'LL NEED SOMEONE ON THE LIGHT SWITCH... ONE VOLUNTEER... YOU THERE, HONEY, GET THE SWITCH!

IS THAT THE BELL ALREADY?

OKAY, WE'LL TAKE IT TOMORROW FROM HERE.. EVERYONE BE IN PLACE BY NINE! THANK YOU, AND GOOD MORNING!

SCHULZ

A Cry
of
Anguish by
One Who's
Been There

"What
can I
do?" she
moaned.

Sometimes it
seemed that
life was just
too much
for her.

Sometimes she felt that it
was no longer possible to
cope with her problems.

She wanted
to go outside,
and scream.

"Augghhaighhrggrhhgii

ghaaghhauggaurahaugh!"

I HAVE JUST
WRITTEN THE
LONGEST SCREAM
IN THE HISTORY
OF ENGLISH
LITERATURE!

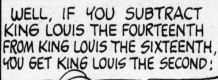

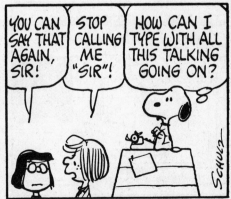

Now is the time for all good men to come to the aid of the country.

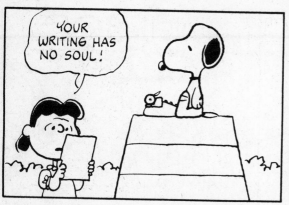

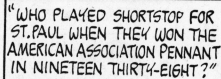

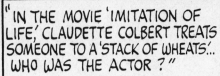

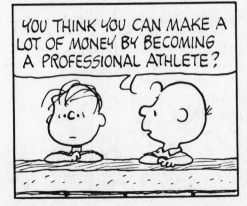

"A MAN HAS TWENTY COINS CONSISTING OF DIMES AND QUARTERS.."

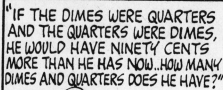

"IF THE DIMES WERE QUARTERS AND THE QUARTERS WERE DIMES, HE WOULD HAVE NINETY CENTS MORE THAN HE HAS NOW..HOW MANY DIMES AND QUARTERS DOES HE HAVE?"

HELP!!!

PRINCIPAL'S Office

SITTING ON THE BENCH OUTSIDE THE PRINCIPAL'S OFFICE IS NOT ONLY DEGRADING, IT'S ALSO DANGEROUS...

EVERY TIME HE OPENS THE DOOR, HE HITS ME IN THE HEAD!

BONK!

A PELICAN?

SOME OF WOODSTOCK'S IMITATIONS CAN GET PRETTY GROSS!

YOU DIDN'T SEND ME A VALENTINE THIS YEAR...

WELL, I GUESS THERE'S ALWAYS NEXT YEAR, ISN'T THERE?

OR THE YEAR AFTER?

SOMETIMES I THINK YOU DON'T REALIZE THAT YOU COULD LOSE ME...

ARE YOU SURE YOU WANT TO SUFFER THE TORTURES OF THE MEMORY OF A LOST LOVE?

DO YOU KNOW THE TORTURES OF THE MEMORY OF A LOST LOVE?

IT'S AWFUL!!!

IT WILL HAUNT YOU NIGHT AND DAY!!

YOU'LL WAKE UP AT NIGHT SCREAMING!

YOU CAN'T EAT! YOU CAN'T SLEEP!! YOU'LL WANT TO SMASH THINGS!

YOU'LL HATE YOURSELF AND THE WORLD AND EVERYBODY IN IT!

OOOOOOO!!!

ARE YOU SURE YOU WANT TO RISK LOSING ME?

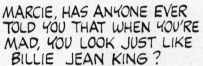

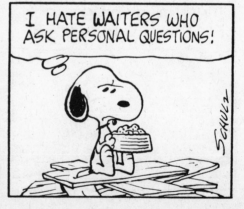